A Window into Story

Poetry by Marilyn Raymond
Images by Cathryn Wellner

Espoir Press
1002 - 1128 Sunset Drive
Kelowna, British Columbia
Canada V1Y 9W7

©2018 Espoir Press

All rights reserved. Poems by Marilyn Raymond and images by Cathryn Wellner may not be reproduced in any format or context, other than in reviews. For any other use, please contact cathryn@cathrynwellner.com.

A Window into Story

978-1-988760-15-5

Table of Contents

Faces of Light	1
The Night Window	5
Blood Moon	6
Freezing	9
Buttercups!	11
In the Woods	12
The Top of the Trail	13
Tangle of Red Willow	14
Morning Coffee	16
Open	18
Sunflowers Singing	20
Hope Moves	22
Revelation	24
A Blue Heron	26
What the Trees Say	28
Beloved Community	
Part I	30
Part II	33
Part III	34
Part IV	35
Credits	36
Meet the book's creators	37

Introduction

This collection of poems spans a quarter of a century. I'm very aware, looking back, I have led a privileged life. My life has been so comfortable and easy in comparison to most beings alive in the world today, perhaps even in any day. Still . . . I have my struggles: pain and loneliness, fear at the damage we are doing to the Earth, and deep sadness at the suffering we cause each other and so many innocent inhabitants of our planet. I chose the poems for the spark of light and hope that each, in some way, contains.

Often my writing begins with walking meditation. I look at the world. Then I go home and write in my living room beside the woodstove. Outside wind and darkness press against the windows; sun and rain fall through the trees; love and sadness and celebration circle close. The interconnected web reveals itself as language.

I believe there exists, under the common fabric of perceived reality, a deeper truth where there are no borders or boundaries and every single thing is part of one great whole. I have an image of lifting a corner of that fabric, where all things and beings are separate, where time is linear, where we live and die as isolated islands of identity, to find an interconnected web so rich and complete that it forms a field of light. In this reality there is no possibility of separation. We all belong, and all that we are contributes to the constantly unfolding creation of the universe.

With this in mind creativity becomes, for me, a sacred act. When I am writing, once I get past the resistance bubble that I always have to struggle free of before I can begin, I find myself in a timeless, compelling, realm of engagement. I feel the interconnected web tugging and shining. Everything is precious.

Working with Cathryn has been a happy experience. I will be forever grateful for the days when an art piece would arrive and we would have short conversations about meaning and design. Her talent and insight have enriched my experience of my poetry. Her art, her presence in my life, and her commitment to our project have been a gift.

Marilyn Raymond

When I first listened to the poetry of Marilyn Raymond, I gasped. Her words marched straight past my barriers and into my heart. That was more than a decade ago, at a service in the Unitarian Fellowship of Kelowna.

I knew then I could never get enough of her poetry. She gave me permission to post seven of her poems on a blog I called "Catching Courage". I treasure and re-read them still. Then she published a chapbook, which I keep handy on a shelf in my living room.

The idea of our doing a book together came slowly. I am a storyteller whose tales are seldom oral these days. Instead, I tell them in blogs and books. It was not until I turned to photography as another means of telling stories that the idea of combining our work began germinating in my mind.

The natural world draws us both. Marilyn writes poems that start in the landscape of the physical world and lead into the landscape of the heart. I take photographs and write micro-stories about the plants, animals, birds, and even fire hydrants I meet on my walks. The Small Scale Stories I post on Instagram and collect in books are a way to give voice to the natural world. A book of Marilyn's poems and my photographs would allow us to weave our stories.

Then Marilyn sent me sixteen of her poems. I read them with ever-deepening amazement and decided what they needed was something more visually complex than straight photographs. So I began playing with photos, textures, and images, experimenting with digital art that would distill some part of each poem's essence.

This book is the result. We are thrilled to share it with you.

Cathryn Wellner

The Path to Gratitude

My small apricot tree,
A volunteer from the compost,
Is beginning to blossom now
Beauty unasked for
Grace after a long, deep winter
I am grateful
And offer praise

Sometimes though
The path to gratitude
Requires the heart risk
Of reaching out to ask for help
When you respond with honest warmth
Beauty blossoms
And I am so grateful

Cathryn and I extend fond gratitude to these friends, our Book Angels, for being first readers and sharing their impressions, compliments, and critiques. The book got better with their feedback.

          Denise Brownlie
          Jan Dawson
          Judith Gunderson
          Suzanne Harper
          Tess Healy
          Kelly Pond
          Dara Tuell
          Joan Becht Willette

Faces of Light

One true thing I know
Everything has another face
Every dark day
        Every sunlit morning
                Every bad news, every smile, every love affair, every death
The world opens and closes itself
        To the rhythm of light and dark
Like eyelids
        Like consciousness....
                A heart beat

The light of soft summer opens
Shines on the blue
Awakens the green
Curls forth in a tiger lily wild rose profusion
And burns it all away
Revealing the bones of her other face
        Anger and wildfire
                Passion gone awry
                      Dry brittle woods
            Ashes and dust.

Leonard says
The light
        Enters through our broken places
        Our wounds,
Through the vulnerability that cracks the shell
My friend says
And also...that's how the light gets out,
        Shining through my willingness to open.

True things are hard to say
    Light opens my eyes to protection and comfort
        Sunlight along the summer trails
            A lantern in the dark
            The gentle nostalgic light of childhood and campfires
            The chalice light shining understanding and connection
            Your smile ~ shining on my heart like a blessing

And then light shows another face
    She reveals my secrets
        She walks me out of the cool shadow
        She drags old pain out of the comforting dark
            And shows me truths I must work hard to welcome
            Squirming wiggling little shames
            Foolish mistakes and hopes
            Failure and grief
            Lines and wrinkles there is no denying
        She walks me out into clarity with all its two sided gifts

Sweet summer light has another face
    And another
        Truth teller
        Nurturer
        Hot passionate lover
        Soft
                Harsh
                      Revealing
        Teacher, healer, friend
        Persephone, Kali, Baba Yaga
            Beautiful and terrible.

Her face begins to soften now as the rhythm plays
 The longest day opens and closes
    And the long evenings begin their lazy tumble into the dark
Summer will blaze and fade
    Loosening her grip
    Letting me rest a little on this journey
    To all the places I must see
        When I shine out
        When the light gets in.

The Night Window

The darkness is watching me
It climbs onto my night table
Crowding the blowsy tulips
Leaning drunkenly out of their small pot
Sucking at the warm yellow petals
    Opened past bearing

In this small circle of light
Under the close warmth of my duvet
Drugs numb the headache
And stillness calms nausea
A tall amaryllis stands reflected in the mirror
    An elegant fading belle

Outside the night window
Dogs bark
Wind shifts uneasily
Snow sifts through shadowed pines
The deep weight of winter
    Drags and grumbles

The woods open up and away
Past the stranger neighbours
To the open forest beyond
The darkness is watching
Night presses
    Against the glass

Blood Moon

Rocks and branches line the windowsills of my dark house
Fossils and clay birds cast dusty shadows
Last night's fire, faded red and gold embers now,
Glows and cracks softly in the stove

David has woken me to come outside
To watch the Blood Moon
Early morning cold wakens my heart and eyes
All the 10 thousand things stand between sun and moon tonight
Changing the light
Making everything strange
Opening a window into story

A small gold curl flares at the edge of the changed moon
Another fire in the night
My mind reaches back to centuries of ancestors
Watching from these familiar hills as the Blood Moon burned
And mystery hung in the Western sky between forever and now

The wooden deck is cold under my bare feet
Our Earth home is blocking the light
Casting shadows of strange on the moon
The cold spring morning wraps me in familiar promise
Of change and return
While the Blood Moon calls me up and out into the dark sky
And deep into more than I can ever understand

We stand close, breathing together into the night
Pine trees sway slowly, creaking their solemn rhythms
The moon shines red above our silent valley

Freezing

A man collapsed in church this morning
His large body swayed and staggered and fell
The shock seized me and I froze

Later a bird flew against my window
The air betrayed her
It reached, with sudden, shocking rigidity
Into the centre of her understanding
And knocked her down

She sat frozen on my deck
I watched her little heart beating dangerously fast
She trembled
After a time she opened her eyes
She stayed very still
I watched her breathing

Who could recover, I thought,
From such a wounding
From such a violent, capricious, incomprehensible NO!

Then she shook herself and flew away

I sat in a sunny place on my deck,
Watching the spring woods
Watching the birds
Thinking of old, cold wounds

I sat quietly
Breathing
Gathering myself together

Buttercups!

Above the long blue lake
Wheel ruts curl up the rise to a small meadow
Filled with last year's grasses

Close to the Earth, Sagebrush Buttercups
Chant their crazy, joyful chorus of colour -
Yellow! Yellow! Yellow!

Generation following generation
They have carried this shining song
To open the year.

And my kind?
We cut that little track of illicit ruts
Through the pine woods

Generation after generation
We left our mark
In the wild and innocent garden

Broken plastic
Red casings of shotgun shells
Sodden piles of toilet paper

Amid elegant shoots of Death Camas
Old newspapers, flaccid and fading,
Argue and whine

Empty stories
Of carelessness and shame
Litter the beautiful hills

And Buttercups shine
Through faded winter grass
Above the long blue lake

In the Woods

Dry woods open softly
Gentle rain rustles the grasses
Robins hunt silently

A wind-downed tree
Reveals torn and twisted flesh
Beautiful and fragrant

In the middle of the trail
Cherry pits and rosehip seeds
Glisten in the steaming pile

Amber pine needles
Gently cover somber grey
Feathers and small bones

The Top of the Trail

Standing at the top of the trail
Through the woods near my home
Sunlight slanting through dark firs
I lift my face, gathering in
The vigorous scent of wet earth
The greening beauty of spring

Morning opens, whispering
Sun darkened shadows stroke
The faded tangle of winter grasses
The tender green feathering close to the dirt
Everyday beauty shivers over my skin
We are familiar partners, these woods and I

Slowly walking the old, mild path to the lake
I watch the seasons turn
Spring after spring I wait for the geese to come home
For the red winged blackbirds and spring peepers
To start singing in the marsh

The woods are almost free
The miracle of belonging yet offers her grace along this trail
Not too visited by the plastic detritus of shallow boredom
The careless damage of strangers

The muddy tracks of ATVs
Have not defeated the chocolate lilies
Or crowded out the meadows of paintbrush

Dusty blue clematis and lady slippers,
The moose and her calf, still hold their secret places
Waiting for silence and slow walkers

Damage and change press their fingers through the years
And still … the trail through the woods
      Takes me slowly and again into everyday beauty
          And the heart opening gift
              Of happiness

Tangle of Red Willow

Son of a Welsh hill farmer
And a woman yearning to be town
You grew up solitary in a family
Of thick stone walls and bitterness

Sullen and silent you grew
Then you up and ran to Canada
Carrying those stone walls in your heart
 A weight too heavy for singing

A burden too lonely for dancing
You grew and the damp stones
Forced their way through your lips
To say - I have never been happy

The echoed weight of it shortens my breath
Never been happy -
But I remember for you
A moment in these smooth Canadian hills

Tromping through a birch grove –
When you stopped
Near a tangle of red willow
And you opened your arms and you whispered

Oh, Canada …
And I was so flooded with tenderness
So filled with a perfect clamoring love
For this land and for you

That I knew
      I knew!
           You must have been
                Weren't you?
                    Happy?

Morning Coffee

I sit outside with my morning coffee
And watch the sun
Spill slowly through the trees
And fill the woods

For a sudden startling moment
My cranberry red bathrobe calls a hummingbird
Its buzzing hover fills my vision
And then it's gone

The bunch grass is fading
Pine trees cast cool shadows
Some of the fir trees are dying
The odd beauty of their red gold tops
Stirs an anxious flurry in my stomach

The air is sweet
And my home nags at me with disquiet
A tension almost like fear
A fear like history

Like the fir trees
There is death in me
I feel it singing through my veins

The August world
Is sunlight and silence ~
A shifting pattern of light and shadow
Shadow and light

Open

My house in the woods is warm at night
The doors and windows encircle
My ordinary life
      A small fire flickers on the hearth

It is peaceful
And quiet
      The world is far away

I am awake this night
Restless
I move through the dark rooms
      Embers glow in the wood stove

I have left the door standing open
Leaves have blown in
Night air slips
Through the dark opening
And wraps long cold fingers
      Around my ankles

Safety is not sure
The other might enter now
The stranger
      The dark lover

Leaves drift over the floor
And the shadow world leans close
      I return, trembling, to my bedroom

What can you do
When passion flows scalding through your tidy fingers
Melts away careful plans
And drips like tears
      Through your breath and your bones

Nothing is ever the same
Nothing is ever the same
When the boundaries are open
      And the dark lover rides in

Sunflowers Singing

Sunflower arrows sing silver green harmony
From sheltered spring hillsides
Their loyal promise of wild yellow hallelujahs
Open doorways to memory and dream

This odd month is out of rhythm
A shrill cold descant ripples above the pale grasses
Winter holds on too long
The frozen lake sounds a deep note of warning

The first people of this land honoured the beauty
That covered these hills with security
Grandmothers taught how to prepare roots
The rhythm of digging, the slow drone of steamig
The hot humming comfort of late winter food

In Seven Generations who will remain
To walk these hills
To hear beauty sing again of warmth and plenty
To be grateful, and repentant?

Will they remember, in the dark of winter,
That cold can be endured
And hunger eased with summer's promise?

Will it be true?
Will the symphony of Earth
Still hold the rhythm of human hearts
And the sweet, high melody of children singing praise?

Hope Moves

A small doorway opens
In a shadowed corner of my mind
A dark eyed child moves hesitantly

Wind blows through winter trees
Dark pines sigh and groan
A heavy river of snow releases
Past crooked limbs and broken places
To the waiting Earth
Branches lift and wave

A frightened woman stands barefoot
On a ridge above a small lake
Summer breeze lifts her hair
Her breathing deepens and pain eases
Her chest opens and softens
Fear releases
The beautiful Earth shares sunflowers
Beneath the dark pines

A child is born at the end of the world
His dark eyes watch carefully
Love surrounds him

Revelation

At the edge of the swamp
The night trails crouch
Curls of invitation stretching off into the bush

Moonlight
Etches shadow fingers through the rushes
My body hums

Silence now…
The frogs hold their breath
Listening for me

Listening…
Slowly, voice by voice, they call me harmless
And their music builds

Rising and weaving
A cradle of song rocks and echoes
Vibrating though my teeth and along my skin

Catching, carrying, until I can almost…
        Almost open
To belief and belonging

In the song charmed night
As the world warms
And darkness beckons

My chest swells and fills with shame and gratitude
For one more spring
Where we are alive together

I try to find hope
In harmless love
At the centre of everything

A Blue Heron

Morning and we are at the river again
Making coffee, cutting onions in Feather's camp kitchen
Twenty years of our river history soothing and disturbing my mind

I thought they would grow old with me, my river friends
Sing at my deathbed, hold me forever
River, of course, had other lessons to teach

A blue heron landed with awkward grace,
All knees and wings, on a large rock in the middle of the amber green river
We stopped making breakfast and watched

He folded himself into his elegant profile
And stood silently above the rushing hush of the river
After a time he lifted himself into the air and flew on

It started to rain, the river changed to gray
And sang a rhythm of rings, interlocking silver
How could I forget this ~ a river is always new

Years and moods of this precious place
Lost faces of friends I have loved echo inside the rain
I'm holding too tightly to the rock

My mind follows the heron up the river
Wild blood flowing silent and perfect
I breathe softly into the morning
Grateful for breakfast and coffee under the rain loud tarp

What the Trees Say

When I'm dead
I'm going to be dead.
I know that from a room with a door

Inside, I'm listening

"Loneliness is the worst and best of things.
That's what the trees say." *

Walking on the Earth
Beside trees and rivers
Opens spaces in my head

On a path through the woods
Sunlight and shadow
Trees murmur seduction and whisper welcome
Dark, underground veins
Pull death into beauty

The silent woods sing -
For everything that has left the room
Lonely, singular
Circumference and centre
- Songs of belonging

I'm listening

*Stan Chung from "Writing and the sonic landscape"

Beloved Community

I
When the moon calls I wish I knew Coyote songs
When she glows, cold and golden, through icy mist
Sketching silver over the grasses and pine trees
I want to lie down in the winter forest and breathe her light
Singing her name into the night

I love the dark
And our beautiful moon ~ littered with space junk
Carrying footprints

One summer night, when the world was young,
Stars and moon shining in warm wet darkness,
I swam out into the night lake along her golden trail
And he was up there, brother of our blood,
Walking the moon path

I love what we know. Wildflowers,
The speed of sound, the texture of moon dust
Everything born of one Mother

In spring I walk carefully through the night
To listen at the edge of the swamp
Waiting to hear frogs
"seekers, calling strange names into the darkness."*
Songs thrilling and echoing, filling the night

I love the mystery ~ of moon and night
Of frog song and fellowship
Everywhere mystery

Smiling in the dark at the edge of their song
I imagine community ~ a sound web of belonging
  A satisfaction so rich that the world is only
This… One… Thing
~ Frogs Singing

* Barbara Taylor Brown from "The Preaching Life"

II
My sisters and I
Kneel on the bathroom floor
beside our half naked Mother

Her fragile skin is soft and shivering
The staple marks, ten days old,
Barely register beside the raw ugliness of a stoma

She looks away from the crush of our awkward
Passionate need to care for her
We wipe her body clean

We measure and cut and read instructions
We press the adhesive firmly against her belly
And hold, one hand hot against the soft curve that once

Held us and one hand firmly against her bum
We hug her close as she looks away
Chin raised, as she has always faced the world

An unlikely reunion, hot, sticky, immediate
Air filled with a rich dense smell of living
Our circle of sisters ~ and Mother, alone at the centre

III
"A whistle of wings in the fading light" *
Raven and kin, sketching a circle that draws me in

A circle of women I believed in
Lost congruency
Changed shape, stopped singing

Coffee after church, the clattering, chatting sound web
With odd pockets of silence and yearning

It has taken me years to learn that community
Is a Baba Yaga answer

Always
And never
The only path

* Cathryn Wellner Facebook comment under a photograph of Canada geese

IV
Around the edges of the room we form a circle
We look inward
The circle is empty

I am alone – living and dying
Grasping at community – the gift wrap around a void
Each mind a small singularity ~ impenetrable awareness

Darkness filled with unknown voices calling strange names
Pain voices, believing voices
The promise of community a flickering candle
I am alone – living and dying

The circle of peace
A dream of connection, solid ground, a changeless sea
We hold it together with our linked hands

A circle of faces
Looking inward and across the space
Of abandoned chairs, scattered hymnbooks

I love what I know of names and stories
We hold together and sing into the void
With warm hands
And shared breath

Singing into the emptiness ~ into the opening
It all falls away, there is only today
And the circle of voices, singing

Credits

Except where noted, all of the textures used as backgrounds and overlays in this book are from the remarkable Denise Love and her 2 Lil' Owls Studio.

Anna Aspnes Designs created the **textures on the Table of Contents and behind the poems on pages 14, 30, 33, 34 and 35.

The title font for the poems is Amelia's Quill. Text is in Bw Surco. Cover fonts are Gorni and Bw Surco. All are licensed through Design Cuts.

My photographs appear on pages 2 (forest on left), 12 (robin), 13 (red-winged blackbird), 21 (sunflowers), 23 (child), 27 (Great Blue Heron), and 29 (forest path).

Other thanks are due to the creators of the elements used in these poems:
- Stuck Circle dancing on the cover and page 34 is from Wikimedia Commons
- Wood texture used on the cover and pages 4, 7, 8 and 19 is from *Moonloop Photography
- Brushes and elements by **Jen Maddocks on pages 2, 12 and 23
- Pixabay photos appear on pages 2, 4, 7, 10, 12, 13, 15, 17, 25, 29, 31, 32 and 33
- Woods on pages 4 and 17 are from **The Colby Files
- The blood moon on page 7 is by Francisco Carlos Calderòn Bocanegra, via Flickr Creative Commons
- Stones on page 7 are from StockUnlimited
- Windows on cover and pages 4 and 7 and the floor and door on page 19 are from Tony Laidig's Scene Builder
- Elements from **Foxeysquirrel can be found on the cover and pages 7, 8, 22 and 28
- Sagebrush buttercup on page 10 is from the Bureau of Land Management, via Flickr Creative Commons
- The woman on page 8 was photographed by **Sebastian Michaels
- The hummingbird on page 17 is by Andrew E. Russell via Creative Commons
- Texture on page 17 by *Nicky Laatz
- Leaves on page 19 are from *MixPixBox
- Texture on page 25 is by *RuleByArt
- Overlay on page 27 is by *ArtistMef (Igor Vitkovskiy)
- The frog on page 31 is by The High Fin Sperm Whale, via Wikimedia Commons
- Frame on page 31 is from *Blixa 6 Studios
- Galaxy texture on page 31 is from *Studio Denmark

All elements are either provided thanks to the generous supporters of the Creative Commons or are licensed through *Design Cuts or **Photoshop Artistry.

Meet the Creators

Marilyn Raymond has been writing poetry all her life—for herself, with her students, for family and friends, and for her church community. She writes as a spiritual practice—a way to deepen her self-awareness and to celebrate connection.

She finds her inspiration in the landscape around her home on the beautiful, unceded territory of the Syilx People. Writing joins her to the "family of things" (Mary Oliver, "Wild Geese") and, beyond that, to the deep mystery. It helps her remember how grateful she is for so much.

Her poems have appeared in two anthologies, *Sacred Circle* and *Sheddings* and in the journal, *Sage-ing*. She has published two poetry chapbooks, *The Void* and *All Shapes All Forms*. Books by Lois Huey Heck and Jim Kalnin (*The Spirituality of Art, The Spirituality of Nature, Going Beyond Words*) include her poems. She also collaborated with artist Lois Huey-Heck on a show called "The Void" at Gallery Vertigo in Vernon, B.C.

Cathryn Wellner's meandering path through life has always been about storytelling. Stories were central to her sequential careers as school librarian, traveling storyteller, and community developer. They were as essential as breath when her expectation to live out her life in the country of her birth, the U.S., became a gypsy's life with stints in France, Germany, the Netherlands, and finally in Canada.

Her pursuit of a good tale has taken three main forms: oral performance, written stories, and, most recently, photography. She has written for print and online sources, published essay collections, contributed to anthologies, created photo books, and compiled a series of Small Scale Stories (combining photographs and micro tales).

Now she is venturing further into the world of digital photography and embraced the chance to collaborate with Marilyn Raymond, whose poetry has long inspired her.

Review this book

If you love this book as much as we do, please share your reaction to it. Post reviews on Amazon and Goodreads and anywhere else you talk about books. Give copies to friends and families. Share it on Facebook, Instagram, Twitter or wherever you hang out online. Your enthusiasm encourages independent creators to continue sharing their visions.

www.ingramcontent.com/pod-product-compliance
Lightning Source LLC
Chambersburg PA
CBHW040004080526
44586CB00027B/2880